Evolving

Under His Umbrella

After the Storm

DAMARIS MEDINA

TRILOGY
A WHOLLY OWNED SUBSIDIARY OF TBN
PROFESSIONAL PUBLISHING MEETS POWERFUL PROMOTION

Evolving Under His Umbrella After the Storm

Trilogy Christian Publishers
A Wholly Owned Subsidiary of Trinity Broadcasting Network
2442 Michelle Drive, Tustin, CA 92780

For information about special discounts for bulk purchases, please contact Trilogy Christian Publishing.

10 9 8 7 6 5 4 3 2 1
Library of Congress Cataloging-in-Publication Data is available.

ISBN 979-8-89333-850-8
ISBN 979-8-89333-851-5 (ebook)

DEDICATION

To Pastor Joseph Santos, a man that loved, lived, taught, and showed Jesus in every way. He was a man that demonstrated his love for Jesus in his marriage. He and his beautiful wife, the amazing woman who is now our Senior Pastor. Both displayed what a God-centered marriage is. Thank you for being a part of my spiritual growth and always pointing me to Jesus.

Pastor Joe's favorite Bible verse, prayed every Sunday to end service:

> *To him who is able to keep you from stumbling and to present you before his glorious presence without fault and with great joy—to the only God our Savior be glory, majesty, power, and authority, through Jesus Christ our Lord, before all ages, now and forevermore! Amen.*
>
> — Jude 24

Go in the peace of our Lord!

— Pastor Joe

INTRODUCTION

Ladies we were created as beautiful, compassionate, loving, gentle nurturers.

I know that we have faced many moments in life that could have altered all that God created us to be in marriage or in our meaningful relationships.

Moment of betrayal and distrust that have brought us to a place of brokenness. Yet God is always waiting, willing, and more than ready to restore us to a place of freedom.

Freedom to boldly be women who show compassion.

Women who love others as themselves.

Women who speak tenderly and gently full of wisdom.

Women who are not afraid to take on a role of a nurturing wife, family member, or friend.

Women who know how to serve as onto the Lord.

Women who know that it takes strength. Strength found in God to live,

Fearfully and wonderfully.

— Psalms 136:14

You will notice that this is a weekly devotional. It is intentionally structured to enable you to take your time and enjoy the journey of evolving. Why evolve? Because we are all a work in progress. We will always be in a progress of becoming better. Not perfect but better. Perfection is promised by God one day.

But, as we wait, we evolve. My prayer is that this weekly devotional will not only increase your faith to walk in love, but also your trust in God pertaining to your interaction in marriage (while waiting for your person or in your meaningful relationships already). That you will be blessed when you are able to see the transformation that will take place in your heart and mind as you lean on God and His Word. I pray that you will not allow yourself to be guided by godless wisdom in being or becoming a strong, godly woman and wife. That you will be unafraid to call yourself by all God has created you to be and know that there is no shame or weakness in submitting yourself to God in a healthy, God-centered life.

> *She is clothed with strength and dignity. She laughs without fear of the future.*
>
> — Proverbs 31:25

My name is Damaris Medina and, just like you, I have a story. I received Jesus as my Savior back in 2003 when I was married to my first husband. However, I did not make a decision to truly begin attending church and serving until 2006. I lived a life that was not pleasing to God, and I felt that in my spirit. I thought being a Christian was just saying "yes" to Jesus and attending Sunday services. Maybe even having some faith for those impossible prayers. In essence, I wasn't walking in the power of His Word. I had distorted thoughts of who I was; I was insecure and afraid. These thoughts would have been transformed with the washing of God's Word **(Ephesians 5:26)**. I have since evolved, and though my thoughts have changed; I have been and still am in the process of allowing

God to replace my daily thoughts with His. I have been married twice, and my view on marriage did not align with God's Word. Though I came to Jesus in my first marriage. I had a worldly view and lifestyle. I had some damage from my first marriage. After my first husband passed away, I was left hurting. I didn't realize how much inner damage I had until my second marriage, and when I realized it, I was already signing divorce papers. I thought the divorce was the worst thing that happened to me.

Actually, the marriage was. I entered into a marriage I didn't pray about and ignored red flags. I came into that second marriage hurt and afraid, and I was left completely broken. If my thoughts were somewhat distorted prior to my second marriage, my view on marriage after the fact was horrific. My total perception on relationships had been altered by the view someone whom I trusted had about me. I wasn't loved gently, protected, and cared for. The words spoken to me were so damaging that I couldn't view marriage as something beautiful and godly. I didn't even trust God enough at this point anymore to submit to Him. I needed a lot of restoration. The Word of God calls us to **"Encourage one another" (1 Thessalonians 5:11).** When God's Word is used to discourage someone (believe me it can be done), you can break someone to a point of total

disbelief in God and themselves. You can bring someone to a place of darkness. That place is full of insecurity, doubt, low self-esteem and confidence in anything, distrust, sadness, and depression. Moreover, you can bring a person to having distorted thoughts of God's unfailing, unconditional love for them. That is the darkest place to enter. That place where you can't believe even God when He says He loves you. Now that can be brokenness to the max. Thankfully, we have a God that will not rest until He can wrap you in His loving

arms, transforms your view, and heal your heart. God is faithful, patient, kind, loving, and merciful. His love brought me to a place of understanding. I realized I was able to experience days of peace, love, and joy. I was able to feel happy without any reason given by someone other than God. I couldn't explain it. Somehow, I just felt it, and I knew it was Him. I know God will continue to do His work on me because, after all, we are all a work in progress until Jesus comes again. But joy has been experienced. I love myself, and I will say something close to what the blind man Jesus healed said. My views were once distorted, but I now understand.

I could have written a book telling my entire story, but I thought: *How much good would that do for another woman who has faced or is currently face to face with a similar pain in need of healing?* A woman who needs to evolve in the power of God's truth. How would telling my side of the story help her? It would only confirm and justify the pain she is already in. Instead, I chose to walk you through the process that has and continues to build me up. That process of regaining, believing, and retaining the beautiful attributes we as women tend to lose when we believe we have lost in love.

WHY EVOLVE?

When you experience brokenness in an ungodly marriage or relationship and are unsure you have been healed from those wounds, you may unknowingly bring them into a new or refreshed God-centered relationship. You may cause damage to your existing meaningful relationships. When that happens you give out only what you possess within. That is why seeking to heal and allow God's truth to change you will help you to establish a strong relationship with God and understand what His Word says about how we are to treat ourselves and others. We must first search ourselves in God. Believe what He says about you and then extend that truth to your spouse or to family and friends. Again, you can only give what you truly possess. If you possess anger, you will give outrage. If you possess unforgiveness, you give out resentment. If you possess selfishness, you have nothing to give. However, when you possess God's truth, mercy, grace, and love, you will learn to **"love your neighbor as you love yourself" (Mark 12:30-31).**

So how do you know you are evolving into a healthy way of being? It is evident in the view you have towards yourself and then towards others. It's evident when you understand the importance of loving yourself as God's beautiful creation enough to speak in love and respect to yourself and others. You will be able to do this with the understanding and strong belief that you and others are God's beautiful creation. We have all been made in His beautiful image.

Many times we say we are healed from past traumas, and you may feel healed. However, you find yourself speaking gracefully to friends and maybe even family members, but as soon as you make a mistake, you tear yourself to shreds. You don't easily forgive yourself, which may cause you to release that unforgiveness in some manner to your loved ones. It is said that we hurt the ones we love most. Mostly unintentionally but we do. Within that "Most" is also you. You know you have come to a place of healing when you can see yourself as precious as God sees you. When you have come to that serene place within yourself, you will know what it means to **"love your neighbor as yourself" (Mark 12:30-31).** Moreover, you will be able to freely give and receive.

NOTE: If you are in an abusive relationship, please know that it is okay to seek help. God intends us to be wise women. Seeking professional help is never an unwise decision. That is my personal opinion, based upon personal experience.

With love,
Damaris

CONTENTS

WEEK 1

Healing to Evolve in Truth

KEY VERSE

And after you have suffered a little while, the God of all grace, who has called you to his eternal glory in Christ, will himself restore, confirm, strengthen, and establish you.

— 1 Peter 5:10

DEVOTIONAL

According to Oxford Languages: "To evolve is to develop gradually, to mature"[1]. The process of healing is to become healthy or sound again, and truth is factualness. In other words, to change into a sound-minded person who is certain.

We know that along with salvation, God also gave us a *"Spirit of love, power and a sound mind" (2 Timothy 1:7).*

According to God's unfailing Word, His Word will change you: "Create in me a clean heart, O God, and renew a right spirit within me" (Psalms 51:10).

1 https://www.oxfordreference.com/view/10.1093/oi/authority.20110810104850102

His Word will heal you: "He heals the brokenhearted and binds up their wounds" (Psalms 147:3).

His Word will cleanse you with truth: "Sanctify them in the truth; your word is truth" (John 17:17).

After all is read, believed, and done, His Word will make you new: "Therefore, if anyone is in Christ, he is a new creation. The old has passed away; behold, the new has come" (2 Corinthians 5:17).

When you have lived in the lie of the distorted truth someone you loved and trusted has fed you, attempting to find the truth becomes difficult. God is love. (1 John 4:19-20) That is a fact. His love will touch your heart with peace and joy. That is a fact. He doesn't ask you to change, His love ushers you into a change. (Romans 12:2) He will never hurt you. (Jeremiah 29:11) He will never lie to you. (Numbers 29:19)

God wants us to love each other: *"This is my commandment, that you love one another as I have loved you" (John 15:12).*

Some have come to the conclusion that walking in your healing means living a life of distrust. Living your life being so cautious that it builds fear in you. Fearful enough not to give your all, of serving, of loving and being loved. That is not walking in truth, that's a life of anxiety. God can give us what we need to be wise. He can give you a discerning spirit. We are told we are to put our trust in God not man: "It is better to take refuge in the Lord than to trust in man" (Psalms 118:8).

You should never have fear in a marriage or in any of your meaningful relationships. You shouldn't fear abiding in the love God commands you to, because you trust in God and should be able to trust in your loved one. It is not to say distrust doesn't exist or could never exist in a relationship. It can and does. Nonetheless, living in a state of distrust, fear, and uncertainty is not living in a healthy relationship: "There is no fear in love, but perfect love casts out fear. For fear has to do with punishment, and whoever fears has not been perfected in love" (1 John 4:18).

> *Love is patient, love is kind. It does not envy, it does not boast, it is not proud. It does not dishonor others, it is not self-seeking, it is not easily angered, it keeps no record of wrongs. Love does not delight in evil but rejoices with the truth. It always protects, always trusts, always hopes, always perseveres. Love never fails.*
>
> — 1 Corinthians 13:4-8

What is a changed, healed heart full of truth? It is freedom. Freedom to put your trust in the one that loves you. Freedom to walk in the condition God created you to walk in. Freedom to be peaceful in giving and receiving love.

> *You keep Him in perfect peace whose mind is stayed on you, because He trusts in you. Trust in the Lord forever, for the Lord God is an everlasting rock.*
>
> — Isaiah 26:3-4

When God's love changes you, it leads you into your healing. Your healing brings you into a place of truth, and in that truth, you come back to a place of love.

JUST A THOUGHT

1 Peter 5:10 does not mean that God is okay with seeing us in our pain. It means He has not turned a blind eye to it. It means that He will, if we allow Him to, heal our hurting hearts and strengthen us and make us whole.

We cannot say how and when God will or will not do, but we believe Him at His Word. We trust that because God's Word does not return to Him empty, we believe Him when He says that He WILL establish us.

> *So shall my word be that goes out from my mouth; it shall not return to me empty, but it shall accomplish that which I purpose, and shall succeed in the thing for which I sent it.*
>
> — Isaiah 55:11

> *God is not man, that he should lie, or a son of man, that he should change his mind. Has he said, and will he not do it? Or has he spoken, and will he not fulfill it?*
>
> — Numbers 23:19

We can trust God to heal us where it is needed. We know that He will do it for His glory, we are fortunate enough to benefit from it. His blessings, grace, mercy, and favor are not just for our own benefit. It is the way we can lead others to Him. That is His glory. When He establishes us, He strengthens us and renews us. Allowing us to be that voice, "In the wilderness prepare the way of the Lord; make straight in the desert a highway for our God" (Isaiah 40).

When we are broken, we are a desert. God comes in to plant a seed of willful change in us that will bear fruit. A fruit of healing and truth. That fruit bearing spirit is the spirit of God's original design for us.

REFLECT, PRAY, JOURNAL

....

....

....

....

....

....

....

....

....

....

....

....

WEEK 2

Faith Intensified

KEY VERSE

So that your faith might not rest in the wisdom of men but in the power of God.

— 1 Corinthians 2:5

DEVOTIONAL

Why faith? Because believe it or not, even when you think you've lost it, it remains your shield. It is your truth guide. Even in your brokenness, faith leads you to the truth in God's Word. Your faith in God can keep you lifted even when a relationship has fallen. Your faith pleases God: "Without faith it is impossible to please him, for whoever would draw near to God must believe that he exists and that he rewards those who seek him" (Hebrews11:6).

Jesus comes in as the ultimate power of faith. He is the giver of faith, so when you come to Him in faith, you are coming to Him with an increased measure of what has been deposited in you by God. We all have a measure of faith, and it is up to us to build it up by way of hearing, studying and applying God's Word. The Word of God says that "*his word will not return to him void" (Isaiah 55:11).* We can then liken it to the fact that because He gave us faith, if we return to Him with increased faith the only thing that can happen is it will produce. It will produce truth, strength, and wisdom. You see, He gives you His Word; when you come back to Him with His Word, it produces. It can "*not return void*" because we know God will not lie. (Numbers 23:19) Therefore, when your faith has increased, you can present your needs to God in prayer. With increased faith, you will push doubt to the side and believe Jesus at His Word when He says, *"And whatever you ask in prayer, you will receive, if you have faith" (Matthew21:22).* Faith in God is what the enemy of our souls is wanting you to lose: *"Be sober-minded; be watchful. Your adversary the devil prowls around like a roaring lion, seeking someone to devour" (1 Peter 5:8).*

If we are not grounded in truth and learn to discern the lies, we fall prey to deceit. We do not use wisdom in what we seek or how we live. Let's not take the Word and misuse it. The Word also says, *"You do not have because you do not ask God. When you ask, you do not receive, because you ask with wrong motives, that you may spend what you get on your pleasures" (James 4:2-3).*

When we ask God for something in prayer, we must also ask ourselves if that which we seek will glorify God or will it be to satisfy our own pleasure? Praying for a husband requires wisdom if you so desire to truly have a God-centered marriage. You can pray for a husband, or you can pray for a spirit-filled man of God. You can pray for someone to speak kindly to you, or you can pray for wisdom in truly knowing, that what is being spoken aligns with God's Word. He will do it. Hold on to your faith in God because we don't ever lose it. We simply give it away. Let's work on increasing our faith so that when we pray, we know we will have what we have asked for. When you feel like you're sinking, your faith can push you through and over the waves to God.

> *For everyone who has been born of God overcomes the world. And this is the victory that has overcome the world—our faith.*
>
> — 1 John 5:4

JUST A THOUGHT

> *Now faith is the assurance of things hoped for, the conviction of things not seen.*
>
> — Hebrews 11:1

Faith is another way of saying that a stronger part of you not only believes *in* God but also believes God. It is not easy, but it is very necessary. It may not feel doable, but it is not impossible. We need faith like we need air. Faith can carry you through any moment. It does not mean you won't have moments. You absolutely will.

> *I have said these things to you, that in me you may have peace. In the world you will have tribulation. But take heart; I have overcome the world.*
>
> — John 16:33

In case you forgot, "take heart" means have faith. Having faith will keep you stronger in seeking God. Your thoughts may lead you to want to give up on having faith for anything. That is when you tell your mind those thoughts are not yours because you "have the mind of Christ" (1 Corinthians 2:16). Love is beautiful when handled properly; however, when it is mishandled or manipulated it can possibly cause us to feel that all faith has been lost. We can make loving someone so much greater than loving and having faith in God. The amazing thing about having a family of believers is that someone will always be used by God to speak into that mustard size faith to make it grow again. God can and will use anyone to bring you back into His love: "As each has received a gift, use it to serve one another, as good stewards of God's varied grace" (1 Peter 4:10). So hold on to your faith, you're gonna need it!

REFLECT, PRAY, JOURNAL

WEEK 3

The Place in Prayer

KEY VERSES

Then you will call upon me and come and pray to me, and I will hear you.

— Jeremiah 29:12

Call to me and I will answer you, and will tell you great and hidden things that you have not known.

— Jeremiah 33:3

DEVOTIONAL

As Christians we know that maintaining our relationship with God the Father through prayer is vital in our walk. Prayer is that quality time spent with God as you allow Him to speak into your spirit. It is that amazing time of being still. Prayer may very well be the time when God works in your heart and mind. The Word says, "Then you will call upon me and come and pray to me, and I will hear you" (Jeremiah 29:12).

How awesome is that! We know that though God spoke this word to Jeremiah, He also means it for us because we know Jesus prayed for all who would believe: "My prayer is not for them alone, I pray also for those who will believe in me through their message" (John 17:20).

When you come to a place of healing, prayer is the most important action you take. Healing is not an easy place to come to but having a consistent prayer life makes the journey beautiful.

We know that Jesus came to reconcile us to the Father. We were estranged from Him at some point, but there is so much God wants to show you. So much truth He wants to reveal, and we know that takes place in His Word, prayer, and receiving sound doctrine. I personally know that when I just didn't have anything to give within me, I prayed, even when I didn't have the words to say.

He heard my heart, read my tears, and allowed me to give Him my pain. It took some time, but the more I prayed the more comfort I began to feel. The more comfort I felt, the more I wanted to be in His presence. The more I stayed in His presence, the more His Spirit showed me what I needed to pray for. The more I prayed, the more in love I fell with God. Prayer is the best thing you can do for yourself and loved ones. It is when you pray that God will work in you and for you. It is in that place in prayer that healing ushers in change and that change leads you to the truth of who you truly are to your Loving Heavenly Father.

JUST A THOUGHT

When you pray, you are entering into a place of tranquility. A place where only you and God are communicating through His Spirit. It is the place where you lay all your burdens, concerns, and anxieties down. It is a place of trust, a place of release. In prayer you can tell God anything without fear. You can seek forgiveness and receive grace. It is the place you can bring all your worries about your marriage, children, family members, friends, and co-workers. We don't know what others are thinking or feeling unless they speak it out. In prayer you can seek the All-Knowing Father to touch the hearts and minds of those who need it. It is the place of comfort and joy. It is the place of certainty. It is where you are certain that God will hear you and respond in His perfect time. It is the place where you can seek transformation within yourself. Don't forget that prayer and faith go hand-in-hand.

> *And whatever you ask in prayer, you will receive, if you have faith.*
>
> — Matthew 21:22

REFLECT, PRAY, JOURNAL

....

....

....

....

....

....

WEEK 4
Producing & Cultivating

KEY VERSE

But the fruit of the Spirit is love, joy, peace, forbearance, kindness, gentleness and self-control.

— Galatians 5:22

DEVOTIONAL

When you seek healing, you make yourself available to produce good fruit. You work at becoming a woman that embodies "the fruit of the Spirit." To embody means to be an expression of or visible form to something. Keep in mind that it is working at becoming. That work is daily. We all have our censored and uncensored moments. The only One Who was able to fully walk in the fruit of the Spirit was Jesus. As your healing transforms you, and you begin to walk in the truth of who God created you to be, you will see the evidence that good fruit show up here and there. If you're unsure of what that looks like, allow yourself to be led by some examples found in the love you have for yourself *(Mark 12:31)*. The joy you find in all that is God *(Psalms 30:11)*. The peace that surpasses understanding *(Philippians 4:6-7).* Developing in patience *(Romans 8:25).* Kindness will be your fashion statement *(Colossians 3:12).* Self-control will be your runway *(2 Timothy 1:7).*

When you begin to develop these attributes as a woman of God you will be better equipped to not only produce but to begin cultivating them in your meaningful relationships.

You may think this is a lot of work and will take time. You're right. It is work, but it is work that provides great benefits. It will take time. We're a work in progress, which means we will always work at exemplifying the love and gentleness of our Savior on this side of heaven. It doesn't mean you won't have some down moments, days when you don't have enough. Moments when you may not feel you can forgive yourself for something. Moments that make you mad, and joy seems like it's light years away. Moments when grace is the name of someone that just pushed your last button. It is in those moments you need to take a deep breath. Remember you are human, and you will make mistakes. Run as fast as you can and seek God's grace for yourself and others so you can move forward.

I always keep in mind what my pastor tells us after every service, "You are the only Jesus, those who come in contact with you will see." No pressure, right? You see, we never have to attempt to walk this Christ-like walk alone. God gave us instructions and details of what His heart is for us. We bear His image and are loved by Him. We only need to seek Him for guidance. He promises that He will fill us with His Spirit so that we will have the capability of typifying Jesus in every area of our lives to our best ability. If you feel you need work in the producing and cultivating department of your relationships, simply ease into the process. You can start by praying for an opportunity that will produce in you even one of these awesome attributes. Work on each attribute until it becomes a part of who you truly are. A strong, loving, joyful, peaceful, patiently kind, and gentle woman of God who can take on each day with self-control.

JUST A THOUGHT

Loosening the soil surface can break up the weed growing cycle, forcing roots to the surface to dry out and die. This reduces competition and allows more nutrients to reach plants. This is the instructions on cultivating land to prepare it to produce.

If your inner being has been so badly wounded you cannot attempt to just suppress it and move on like you were never affected, you have to uproot and face whatever caused you pain. If someone caused you pain, you cannot change them. You can only work on healing yourself. The Word says "Neither is new wine put into old wineskins. If it is, the skins burst, and the wine is spilled and the skins are destroyed. But new wine is put into fresh wineskins, and so both are preserved." (Matthew 9:17)

When you have come to a place of understanding the true value of "The fruit of the Spirit," you understand why healing is necessary in order for you to walk in wholeness. If you suppress your previous hurt and disappointments, you will burst out. You will not be able to maintain a healthy relationship with unhealthy thoughts caused by a previous one. However, when you have laid down your burdens and allowed God to do the work much needed in you, you may even have the capability of being aware of bad fruits or maybe even extracting the good in others by allowing God to work in and through you. If you are impatient with your children, aggravated with your spouse, or unhappy in your workplace, you can step aside and allow God to cultivate that soil in these areas, simultaneously allowing God to continue the "good work he has begun in you" (Philippians 1:6).

Only God can do cultivate difficult soil in us and others to become producers of His good fruit. Do not allow anything to take your eyes off God. Not to say it won't happen but when it does, refocus!

REFLECT, PRAY, JOURNAL

WEEK 5
The Power of Words

KEY VERSE

Anxiety in a man's heart weighs him down, but a good word makes him glad.

— Proverbs 12:25

DEVOTIONAL

Communication is vital. I'm sure you already know this. However, what some are not aware of is how important communication is in a close relationship and especially in marriage. Communication is an art in marriage that requires the following tools to properly craft: time set aside, attentiveness, understanding, compassion, and respectful feedback. Communication does not require the following: dismissive approach, yelling, disdain, hurtful words, or the silent treatment. When you add a dose of love as you communicate with a loved one, it opens a door to unity, respect, appreciation, trust, confidence, and strength. Allowing someone to openly express their concerns and wants in a loving approach makes way for someone to feel they can trust you enough to be vulnerable.

Something many women feel is definitely a place they have not been invited to enter in their marriage or meaningful relationships. As women, we sometimes need reassurance that we matter to our spouses or even our friends. Communication welcomes that reassurance. I know that when we come home from work, we want to vent even when sometimes nothing much has occurred in our day. Communicating it to someone you love sometimes helps you feel validated. We must also be mindful to extend that same attentiveness when someone we love desires to be heard. Communication is not only for venting or expressing concerns. It is very important that we take a moment or two to use our God-given voice to encourage others in need of it. Part of the healing journey will require occasional uplifting from others and you doing the same for others. Let's not ignore the fact that God created us to be relational beings. We establish a relationship with him and with those we love. The Word of God instructs, *"Therefore encourage one another and build one another up, just as you are doing" (1 Thessalonians 5:11).*

Effective communication within marriage is a form of intimacy. It is building a close relationship, close attachment, close friendship, and companionship. We cannot be afraid to build this close relationship with our spouses, and we can learn to take a few minutes every so often to reach out to loved ones. If your thoughts and feelings have been dismissed, pray for the courage to open the lines of communication in any area of your life. We cannot allow our past to interrupt a healthy future in creating togetherness. Remember in marriage, communication allows your spouse to learn about your needs and allows you to learn about your husband's needs. It allows you to gain a greater understanding of those you fellowship with. Lacking effective and healthy communication in marriage will cause estrangement. It will cause your meaningful relationships to become distant. Take some time to put the distractions to the side and build that connection. Listen to each other; learn more about each other. We know our lives can be so busy we would rather text a loved one instead of taking a few minutes to simply say hello. It is truly a blessing when you take some time to connect. We have become so accustomed to technology that the connection is not the same. When it comes to communication, let's get back to basics, which means using your phone to actually talk or putting it away to enjoy a private conversation.

JUST A THOUGHT

When I think about going back to basics, I think about the times when cell phones were not easily accessible. A time when some families could only afford one television at home and when play time was using actual toys and not video games. It was a time in which we communicated face to face. It helped to make some families stronger and united. That old fashioned manner of communication could become rare. The beauty of spending time in communication with a loved one is having the ability to learn them so well, they won't have to say a word in order for you to know what they may be thinking. Technology is extremely helpful to us in many ways. However, we have allowed technology to take over the innocence and beauty of unity.

So then let us pursue what makes for peace and for mutual upbuilding.

— Romans 14:19

REFLECT, PRAY, JOURNAL

WEEK 6

Bountiful Grace

KEY VERSE

And God is able to make all grace abound to you, so that having all sufficiency in all things at all times, you may abound in every good work.

—2 Corinthians 9:8

DEVOTIONAL

According to Oxford Languages, grace means: "elegance, charm, poise, finesse, stylishness, ease and effortlessness." Being graceful sometimes takes practice. Sometimes a lot of practice. Life sure knows how to beat the grace out of you.

It is possible in marriage to feel like grace has been stripped from you. You may wonder: *How exactly?* Well, when you are not treated with gentleness, you may already battle with insecurity. If your husband treats other women more delicately and is generous in his compliments to them while you get nothing or he ignores how much work you put into your hair or make-up, you won't feel noticed.

But God, being all merciful and graceful, can refuel your grace tank when you're running on empty. When He does, we must extend that grace to others. Without exception or conditions. Especially to yourself. God says He "is able to make all grace abound in you" (2 Corinthians 9:8). When you come to the conclusion of what that truly means, it is truly worth seeking His grace and allowing Him to transform you.

He is able to transform you into being a woman who speaks, walks, and conducts herself with elegance, charm, poise, and finesse.

It will take prayer and practice, believe me. The fact is, we will deal with different personalities, some pleasant and others not so pleasant. In any case, we maintain our gracefulness and extend it wherever it is needed. God's Word is full of love. He extends grace sufficient enough to pour out to others. We read in the Gospels how people sought Jesus as He went from place to place. I strongly believe it was the grace in which Jesus walked in that attracted many. In the many roles we take on in our lives as women, we can do it all with grace. We can be a graceful wife, a graceful family member, a graceful friend. Especially if we seek to win the hearts of those we love to Christ. We must be graceful. Grace may have been one of the traits that caught your husband's attention when he first saw you. The graceful way in which you walked or the graceful way in which you spoke to him. Don't let that go! Remember in your marriage you are the Jesus your husband sees daily. Let him see that benevolence in you in every interaction you have with him. When you find it difficult to extend grace, don't forget you are not the one that can produce grace, but you can learn to cultivate it. Extending grace to your loved ones is extending the grace much needed and required in cultivating strong, God-centered relationships. If you find yourself giving more than what you're receiving, keep on giving because God takes notice, and the one who produces grace will be the one to extend it where it is lacking.

> *Give, and it will be given to you. Good measure, pressed down, shaken together, running over, will be put into your lap. For with the measure you use it will be measured back to you.*
>
> — Luke 6:38

JUST A THOUGHT

Grace is not the easiest thing to give. When extending grace to others, it takes what we have inside of us. However, what you have inside is given to you by God. If you're having a rough day at work and a moment presents itself where you must extend grace, it can feel tedious. However, keeping our minds in grateful mode can really make a difference.

Remain grateful that we do not have to do anything to earn God's grace. It is freely given. We don't want to live our lives in constant remembrance of when God's grace pulled us out of our mess, but having the grateful attitude of when and how He did can be of great benefit in order to extend that much needed grace. Be generous with grace, because it was generously extended to you.

> *But if it is by grace, it is no longer on the basis of works; otherwise grace would no longer be grace.*
>
> — Romans 11:6

And whatever you do, in word or deed, do everything in the name of the Lord Jesus, giving thanks to God the Father through him.

— Colossians 3:17

REFLECT, PRAY, JOURNAL

WEEK 7

Honor One Another

KEY VERSE

Love one another with brotherly affection. Outdo one another in showing honor.

— Romans 12:10

DEVOTIONAL

Honor is another word for respect. It is something that seems to be lacking among so many areas in this era. I remember hearing wedding vows as a child, and the vows always included "to honor, respect, and obey." As the years have passed, many couples have removed those words from their wedding vows. I can definitely understand how those words can be misused in a marriage. I personally experienced the misuse of those words in my previous marriage. However, I haven't stopped believing that they are valuable and can have a positive impact in meaningful relationships when we truly understand them. To respect someone means to have admiration and esteem for that person. To honor is have high respect, and to obey is to carry out what has been promised.

In essence, you respect your spouse, honor your commitment, and carry out your vows with integrity. I'm sure that reading what Ephesians 5:33 has to say can raise some eyebrows, but let's read it anyway: *"However, let each one of you love his wife as himself, and let the wife see that she respects her husband."*

That verse states clearly the wife is to respect the husband, but the husband is required to love his wife. It goes hand-in-hand. When you respect your husband, it is an unspoken action that says you love him, and when your husband demonstrates love for you, he is honoring his commitment to God and you.

If you are a single woman still waiting for your husband, this verse is also for you pre-marriage. God says the man is to "love his wife as himself." Clearly, if you see a man that does not show love and respect for himself, you are able to know that this may not end as happily as you would want it to. In a case such as that, reconsider and don't take something God would not give you. It is also very important to walk with self-respect. I have come to believe that people will respect what and who you respect. Let's keep in mind, we can only give what we have. When you respect yourself, you can respect others, and you can honor commitments with integrity.

JUST A THOUGHT

Aretha Franklin sure knew what she wanted and spelled it out. We all want to be respected. We want our opinions, desires, and way of being to be viewed with respect. The question is, are we respecting ourselves enough to demonstrate that to others? In other words, are you demonstrating respect towards yourself? Do you honor your own opinions and way of being?

Are you conducting yourself in an honorable manner behind closed doors? You won't have to demand respect if you walk in self-respect. When honor and respect become part of your way of being, it will show, and you can demand it gracefully, sometimes without asking for it. Especially when you show respect for others as well.

> *So whatever you wish that others would do to you, do also to them, for this is the Law and the Prophets.*
>
> — Matthew 7:12

REFLECT, PRAY, JOURNAL

WEEK 8

Noble-Mindedness

KEY VERSE

Her husband has full confidence in her and lacks nothing of value.

— Proverbs 31:11

DEVOTIONAL

I often wonder if the Proverbs 31 woman ever felt the pressure of being such an excellent woman, wife, mother, and entrepreneur. She is so put together, selfless, tender, loving, and authentic. A woman of grace and integrity. She sounds so refined yet strong and fearless. She is a trustworthy woman in her marriage: *"Her husband has full confidence in her and lacks nothing of value" (Proverbs 31:11)*. When we see the Word valued, some may automatically associate it with material value. However, the Word of God refers to *"value"* as that which is priceless. When we consider the attributes of the Proverbs 31 woman, we must consider them all. Everything about being a woman of excellence was described in her. Including the fact that she was a trustworthy wife, a wife her husband could feel completely safe with. He did not belittle her; in fact, it states,

"Her children arise and call her blessed; her husband also, and he praises her" (Proverbs 31:28).

This passage tells me that her husband is grateful about the fact that he knows he can put his full trust in his wife because she honors her marriage and her home. She is incorruptible, incapable of being false. She is a woman who does not assume or jump to any conclusions. She listens, allows others a fair opportunity to explain, and takes others' points of view into consideration. She puts her trust in God.

She is loyal, respectful, honest, fair, and trustworthy. Her husband knows that his wife seeks God for every area of her life, and he honors her. Becoming this type of woman may be a desire for some of us; however, in the back of our minds, we fear it. Why? Simply because some men do not know how to value these attributes in a woman. But becoming this woman of excellence cannot be done for anyone else but God and you. Attempt it anyway. It will not happen overnight. It is a journey that you take with God to allow Him to mold you into this type of woman. It takes time to implement it all, but start small. It can be difficult, but take your time and focus on the small acts. It is the small things in life that can grow to be wonderful, resilient, and lasting. Working on becoming an incorruptible woman is a big deal. Being considered reliable amongst family and friends speaks volume about you.

Let integrity be who you are for yourself and those you love.

JUST A THOUGHT

How can you tell you have become a woman of integrity? Well, a virtuous woman maintains godly moral standards. She is gracefully disciplined. She does what she says and sets herself out to do.

She honors her word and gives others the benefit of doubt. She values time and relationships. She is not wasteful. She has learned how to use the bad for good. She allows herself the space to be human.

She doesn't pretend she has it all together. She is honest first with herself and then with others. She has learned how to differentiate between what she can change and what she needs to surrender to God.

She is learning to truly love herself. She is learning that rejection is not her name. She has learned that she is not a victim, but she is victorious. She works daily at keeping her head up because she knows that everything she needs, God will supply.

> *May integrity and uprightness preserve me, for I wait for you.*
>
> — Psalms 25:21

REFLECT, PRAY, JOURNAL

WEEK 9

The Chains of Resentment

KEY VERSE

Be kind and compassionate to one another, forgiving each other, just as in Christ God forgave you.

— Ephesians 4:32

DEVOTIONAL

Forgiveness. A remarkable chain breaker. This is not something you haven't heard before. It's been said that forgiving yourself and others gives you back peace from within. It really is true. Not easy but true. Forgiveness is a loving and difficult thing to do simultaneously. It takes loving God and yourself enough to forgive. See, when you love someone, you want to be kind to the ones they love. Forgiveness is an act of kindness that is compelled by love for God. It also takes realizing love for yourself enough to free yourself from the chains of resentment, those chains that can paralyze your life. It is very difficult because the pain we have endured from the hurt someone caused, and in our frail human sense, we want the one who hurt us to hurt twice as much. You honestly feel in that hurting moment that it will give you a sense of satisfaction. Honestly, it doesn't and never will. When God is working in you, He gives you a *"heart of flesh" (Ezekiel 26:36).*

That heart beloved will not want to see another person feel the pain you have felt. That is what God will do in you.

Forgiveness allows you to move forward, and it allows God to continue the *"good work in you" (Philippians 1:6).* There isn't anyone that has not failed. We all have (see Romans 3:23). Yet, we seek forgiveness in God and in His abundant mercy, and He forgives us.

Extending mercy is what you're doing when you forgive. If you hold on to unforgiveness and become resentful, it may very well control your actions towards others. The actions you take will not be done out of logic but pain. That pain can cause you to live your life in a state of defensiveness, anger, and bitterness. Being in that constant state will cause you to unknowingly respond angry and can extend hurt to your marriage or other meaningful relationships.

Resentment is a seed planted in your heart and grows slowly but eventually takes full control. When that happens, we have given way to the enemy of our souls to utilize that seed within us to make others stumble as well as ourselves. It truly does cause a domino effect despite how much we justify holding on to resentment. We need not to ever forget that when someone attempts or actually does cause us pain, it is only a reflection of the pain they themselves are holding on to. We tend to give only what we have enough of. Resentment can also blind you of discernment; we need it so that we can be alert to whom we open our hearts. We don't have to walk in fear. We just need to be mindful.

"Be sober-minded; be watchful. Your adversary the devil prowls around like a roaring lion, seeking someone to devour."

— 1 Peter 5:8

Make a decision to release any unforgiveness you may be holding onto. Set yourself free to walk in the power of love, peace, joy, and forgiveness. That goes for you, if you are holding on to something you think you cannot forgive yourself for, it's time to think again and forgive yourself so that you can walk in freedom from it.

Before you can learn to forgive others, you have to learn to forgive yourself.

JUST A THOUGHT

I remember holding on to unforgiveness like it was my security blanket. It really wasn't keeping me warm. However, one day I realized (or God opened my eyes to see rather). That every time someone spoke to me about my ex-husband, I felt like I wanted to start shadow boxing. Who was I fighting against? There was no one in front me. Let go of unforgiveness or else you will get worn out shadow boxing against nothing.

For we do not wrestle against flesh and blood, but against the rulers, against the authorities, against the cosmic powers over this present darkness, against the spiritual forces of evil in the heavenly places.

— Ephesians 6:12

REFLECT, PRAY, JOURNAL

WEEK 10

Harmoniously Minded

KEY VERSE

Complete my joy by being of the same mind, having the same love, being in full accord and of one mind.

— Philippians 2:2

DEVOTIONAL

You may find that your giving tank may occasionally empty while putting in your labor of love and *"doing all things as onto the Lord" (Colossians 3:23).* It truly is generous of you, but it would be nice to experience reciprocation from your husband, family members, and/or friends. It can become a bit heartbreaking to give all you can into a relationship and never experience the same grace, appreciation, or gestures. If you're experiencing that with your husband, it's possible that he is not perceiving the same and quite possibly believes he is doing his part in the marriage. The same can be said with friends and family. Remember we are not mind readers. Therefore, effective and graceful communication can open the doors to expressing your feelings. In doing so, you may be helping your loved one see that you are not feeling valued. God's Word calls us to be of the same mind.

Marriage is a unity, which means togetherness. It does happen within family and friends where one gives more than another. Many of us experience situations such as those; however, bringing it to

someone's attention in a manner that causes them to feel defensive will not result in a harmonious agreement. We are reminded that God instructs us to have *"the same love" (Philippians 2:2).* The thing is, if someone is not matching your energy, you have to match Jesus' energy. It will not be easy, but this is not a sprint. It is a journey and not one that will take minutes or hours. It will take time, but God does not turn a blind eye to the willing and obedient soul. God will reciprocate the grace you give out. If the case is that you are the one not matching an energy of love and peace, then it may very well be time to reconsider and unite yourself with a loving and harmonious spirit. Incorporate this in you, carry yourself with the same mind that is in Christ Jesus.

JUST A THOUGHT

> *And above all these put on love, which binds everything together in perfect harmony.*
>
> — Colossians 3:14

We often hear people say you have to be the bigger person. We may think that pertains to forgiveness, but in reality, it applies to every area of our lives. When you are attempting to discuss a matter at home with your spouse or a family member and you are not seeing eye-to-eye, you may very well have to be the one to come to the conclusion to agree, to disagree. If a situation arises at work where you can dispute or just keep quiet and let

God fight a battle for you, you may very well have to be the one to remain quiet and let God do your bidding. It is not always easy, and we won't always have the same perspective on all things; however, you being rooted in Jesus and His Word. You can rest assured that you do have someone who does see eye-to-eye with you.

> *If you abide in me, and my words abide in you, ask whatever you wish, and it will be done for you.*
>
> — John 15:7

REFLECT, PRAY, JOURNAL

....

....

....

....

....

....

....

WEEK 11

Agreeable Reception

KEY VERSE

Therefore let us stop passing judgement on one another.

— Romans 14:13

DEVOTIONAL

Why is it that when we first fall in love, we find absolutely no faults in our person? Then, as soon as we are married, everything they do boils our blood and clogs our arteries. We bring out our judges note pad and start making notes of the things that need changing yesterday. Why do we do that to our loved ones? It is always easy to find fault in someone else but rarely examine ours.

God never asks us to change before we come to Him. If He points out our flaws, it is because those flaws are harmful. For the most part He accepts us, and it is His grace that causes us to want to become better and work on our flaws.

We know there are bad habits we can change that can cause damage to ourselves and meaningful relationships. Some habits require guidance and support. For the most part, many of us seek to mold someone else into something we ourselves think is adequate or accepting. That can be detrimental to a relationship.

I have heard many people say the one thing they love about their spouse is the fact that he/she accepts who they are. For example, if your spouse enjoys eating chocolate soon after dinner and you chose to be more health conscience. There is no harm in that. Despite the many things you may have in common, there will be the many you just don't and won't. Why make him change that about him? If he was never much of a communicator when you were dating and you never bothered to address it then, why change him after marriage? Accepting someone for who they are is a beautiful gift to give someone you love. It allows them to love themselves as well. It doesn't make them feel like there is something severely wrong with them or cause them to feel inferior.

God welcomed you with open arms, and He didn't force you to change. He loved you unconditionally, and it was that unconditional love that brought about the change in you. When you want to change someone in your relationship, start with you. You can change your perspective and learn to love and accept others for who they are, especially your spouse.

JUST A THOUGHT

Who ever said that change is bad? Change can be good and should always be welcomed. As long as it is a positive change that will contribute to unity, prosperity, joy, love, and peace. That kind of change should never be delayed. If you feel your relationship is in a state of disunity, you don't have to accept that. You can do your graceful due diligence to bring about unity. You may not feel that you need to change anything about you. If that is your story and you want to stick to it, then so be it, you are in all your God given right to feel how you do. However, you cannot want to remain the same and find the flaws in others. No one is perfect, including you. I apologize for being so harsh with that one. Sometimes the truth is just straight, and it cannot be curved. We are not in the place of God. If God Himself allows us room to voluntarily seek Him for change within ourselves, we must know our place and be still as God Himself works out the details. We are called to lead in love and if something requires changing, we allow God to first work in us and then that which concerns us.

> *Casting all your anxieties on him, because he cares for you.*
>
> — 1 Peter 5:7

REFLECT, PRAY, JOURNAL

....

....

....

....

....

....

WEEK 12

Extremities

KEY VERSE

For I do not mean that others should be eased and you burdened, but that as a matter of fairness your abundance at the present time should supply their need, so that their abundance may supply your need, that there may be fairness.

— 2 Corinthians 8:13-14

DEVOTIONAL

Boundaries is another very important element in the healing process. Boundaries is a crucial element in any relationship. Boundaries can be likened to part of the structure that helps in sustaining the foundation. There are several types of boundaries. Here are just a select few:

- physical
- intellectual
- emotional
- and time

We must learn to set boundaries others are to respect and we are to respect the boundaries set by others. In doing so you will be able to benefit from a mature, healthy relationship. We don't usually set boundaries with our friends right at the start of our friendship. When you have a childhood friendship your friend learns everything about you and your boundaries. The respect isn't always explained, it somehow grows with you. However, that is not always the case as some people really don't care to pay attention to that. Jesus said, *"Let what you say be simply 'Yes' or 'No'; anything more than this comes from evil" (Matthew 5:37).*

In other words, respect someone's decisions which falls into intellectual boundaries. As we read 2 Corinthians 8:13-14, it is in essence telling us that in a relationship a mutual giving in abundance will allow the needs of others to be supplied. It makes perfect sense when you read it meticulously.

Let's say in marriage when you give high regard to your spouse's intellectual, emotional, and time boundaries. Your spouse's needs would have been abundantly supplied that he can give back. It may not sound fair that you have to give before he does but what you are doing in the event he hasn't, is simply setting an example. You are also showing respect towards your boundaries. In the end it is beneficial. In time boundaries, when you set aside enough time for each facet of your life and have learned to have balance, you have supplied the need of quality time.

Of the boundaries mentioned previously, it is important to always respect emotional, intellectual, and physical boundaries. It is when you belittle or undermine your spouse that you are crossing the fine line of the boundaries that require mutual respect. We are well aware of women and men who have experienced physical abuse. We know those boundaries have been crossed to a point of no return.

God is a God of order. Let's follow the example of Jesus in being respectful of our loved one's boundaries. In doing so you are showing the love of Christ in your relationships.

JUST A THOUGHT

Boundaries are that which we teach our children when they attempt to touch something. We say, "No don't touch." We are teaching them that touching something that can hurt them is not good.

When they are adolescents and want to stay up late, we set boundaries. Staying up past bedtime during a school week will not allow them to register what is being taught.

We set healthy boundaries for our loved ones. We need to learn that we are worth having healthy boundaries that we honor so others will to.

You may have experienced an unhealthy relationship in which you were not setting boundaries. That may have caused a lot of hurt to you, but you learn and keep on taking those steps found in God's Word to build you up. Setting healthy boundaries is a way you show yourself how much you love yourself.

Again, respect your boundaries, and others will also.

> *Let each of you look not only to his own interests, but also to the interests of others.*
>
> — Philippians 2:4

REFLECT, PRAY, JOURNAL

WEEK 13
Understanding

KEY VERSE

Whoever is slow to anger has great understanding, but he who has a hasty temper exalts folly.

— Proverbs 14:29

DEVOTIONAL

Having understanding is another word for discernment, which we know means having the ability to judge well. When you begin evolving as you heal, having understanding allows you to not only exercise discernment but also compassion towards others. You understand that others may act in ways or say things that may very well come from a place of pain. Many times exercising that ability is not easy. In meaningful relationships having the ability to judge well can be very beneficial. Your loved one may express something that simply is not clear to you. They may act in a manner in which you don't understand. However, when we lack the ability to understand we need to make sure we are not judgmental. Despite the fact that having discernment means to judge well. That does not mean we are to judge someone; rather, we can approach the misunderstanding with compassion by first listening well and then carefully inquiring. We should be careful not to ever express our own misinterpretation in such a way that can hurt others and our relationships.

> *A fool takes no pleasure in understanding, but only in expressing his opinion.*
>
> — Proverbs 18:2

We will not always concur with others. When we don't, we respectfully move on. God has much to say about understanding. It is what He wants us to attain. We know that we understand what is right and what is wrong however, in our daily dealings with our loved ones we can become easily irritated all due to a simple lack of misunderstanding them or how they express themselves.

> *Whoever restrains his words has knowledge, and he who has a cool spirit is a man of understanding.*
>
> — Proverbs 17:27

When we seek for understanding He gives us clarity about His Word, about the love we are to walk in, about having self-control, about being selfless and the way we are to approach others. God's Word is full of knowledge, and if you seek to have the ability to understand others and their why, you are making room to broaden your understanding and perspective. Let the wisdom God's Word freely gives you lead you to an understanding that will guide you.

Let the wise hear and increase in learning, and the one who understands obtain guidance…

— Proverbs 1:5

JUST A THOUGHT

Have you attempted to learn a new language? You not only have to learn to speak it but also understand what you are learning.

You don't want to learn Spanish without understanding what you're saying. You may possibly tell someone they smell bad when you thought you were telling them how nice their shoes are. That, beloved, would be horrifically awkward.

For the Lord gives wisdom; from his mouth come knowledge and understanding.

— Proverbs 2:6

God wants us to be filled with understanding of His Word and our walk with Him. He wants us to understand that He loves us and that He wants us to prosper and live a life full of wisdom. He does not want us to live this once in a lifetime here on earth foolishly.

Let's seek understanding in God's love and grace so that we too can learn to understand others and demonstrate God's love to them through our understanding.

REFLECT, PRAY, JOURNAL

WEEK 14
Humble & Considerate

KEY VERSE

Do nothing from selfish ambition or conceit, but in humility count others more significant than yourselves.

— Philippians 2:3

DEVOTIONAL

We woman sure enjoy a Spa day, the nail salon, and making reservations. It's when we get waited on hand and foot. Who doesn't enjoy having things done for them? The only thing about that enjoyment is it costs money. We can't simply walk into a spa and request that out of the kindness of their hearts they oblige to serving us knowing they will not be receiving payment or even a tip.

Serving is not always something we like to do, especially when we don't receive a tangible reward for it. We don't always find it easy to call ourselves servants. The amazing truth is our Lord had absolutely no qualms with serving or calling Himself a servant.

For even the Son of Man came not to be served but to serve, and to give his life as a ransom for many.

— Mark 10:45

Take a moment to ponder that thought. Jesus—King of kings, Lord of lords—left His deity to become a servant. How many of us would leave such a powerful position to serve others? I'm pretty sure none of us would even think it. However, we follow the example and lead by example. That is exactly what Jesus did. He led by example, teaching us exactly how to live humbly.

We all have a purpose in life, and living it selfishly is not one of them. We are to esteem others and serve in any capacity that we can. For example, a mother serves to the needs of her children, and she does it with love. A wife serves to the needs of her husband, and the husband serves to the needs of his wife. Again, compelled by love. Our purpose at our jobs is to fulfill the needs of that position. In that case it is not always compelled by love but by the need to work. It is not always pleasant as some of us may not enjoy the work we do. But God is calling us to serve our purpose humbly and to do it in love.

We are also reminded that when we count and esteem others more than ourselves, we are doing so onto God.

Truly, I say to you, as you did it to one of the least of these my brothers, you did it to me.

— Matthew 25:40

It is not to say that you forget about yourself. It means you consider yourself and others.

I remember working as a cashier at a deli when I was in my twentys. As the cashier, my job duties included preparing the coffee, maintaining the area of beverages cleaned, emptying out the trash, and doing it all with a smile and pleasant demeanor. That pleasant demeanor would not remain so pleasant when someone would look down on me and with their attitude belittle me. However, I would have to remind myself that I really needed that job and the pay was in fact very good. Why would I let someone who thought themselves to be better than me affect my pay? With that thought in mind, I would compose myself and continue greeting and serving where needed.

When I received Jesus as my Savior, I realized that the pay He offered, no employer will ever have the ability to compete against. He offers unconditional love, mercy, and grace, and eternity is just the icing on that ginormous cake. Let's serve in humility and love, not looking at anything else except the fact that Jesus did it first and because He loved us first.

We love because he first loved us.

— 1 John 4:19

REFLECT, PRAY, JOURNAL

....

....

WEEK 15

The Beauty of a Joyful Heart

KEY VERSE

A joyful heart is good medicine, but a crushed spirit dries up the bones."

— Proverbs 17:22

DEVOTIONAL

It's not easy to be in a constant state of joy. In some cases, finding something to be joyful about can be difficult. We do live a life in which many things can and will bring us sorrow and brokenness. Moreover, how can you break through a laugh if you're drowning in your own tears. Jesus reminds us that, *"I have said these things to you, that in me you may have peace. In the world you will have tribulation. But take heart; I have overcome the world" (John 16:33).*

Clearly, we have been forewarned, but then we have also been instructed to *"Rejoice always" (1 Thessalonians 5:16).*

Talk about being tossed to and from! But when God instructs us, He will provide. He will provide you with joy to replace your sorrow.

Weeping may tarry for the night, but joy comes with the morning.

— Psalms 30:5

When you face moments of sadness and weakness during your process of healing. Those are the moments when you seek for the "joy of the Lord to be your strength" (Nehemiah 8:10, paraphrased).

God will not fail you. God promises He will comfort us, and we trust and not only believe in Him but, believe Him for it. Having a joyful spirit, a good humor, and pleasant disposition is not only attractive but also welcoming to those you love and shifts your atmosphere. Remember we are called to be light, and we know that light brightens up a room. The same is true with a joyful attitude. That joyful attitude is to be present in your everyday at home, work, and fellowship. You never know who you may bless with your smile and joyful, approachable attitude. It is also an attitude that takes less energy from you and brings confusion to the enemy of our souls. The beauty of your joyful heart is just another amazing attribute to who you are.

Let that joyful spirit shine, and don't dim it.

JUST A THOUGHT

Joy, a word that goes a long way when we think of it. Living in a constant state of joy would mean that every element that produces joy for you is absolutely perfect. We know that is not always the case since those elements pertain to spiritual, mental, emotional, relationship, physical, environmental, financial, and occupational health. We will never have all these elements aligned so perfectly that nothing can interrupt our joy. When God tells us to be joyful, He is saying to be joyful in Him because He is greater than anything. He is the giver of joy.

> *May the God of hope fill you with all joy and peace in believing, so that by the power of the Holy Spirit you may abound in hope.*
>
> — Romans 15:13

If our spiritual element, that element that keeps us connected to God is not aligned with God. Then, any other element would only bring you temporary joy. If any of them are tampered with, and they will be, then your joy will never be complete.

> *I have said these things to you so that my joy will be in you and your joy will be complete.*
>
> — John 15:11

In your time alone with God, make sure that the beauty of your joy comes from the Spirit of the living God and not from man, the environment, or even you. Let your joy come from the abundance of God so that you may, "Rejoice in the Lord always; again I will say, rejoice" (Philippians 4:4).

REFLECT, PRAY, JOURNAL

CONCLUSION

I pray you have enjoyed your journey as you evolve and heal in God's truth. We can be very vulnerable as women. Remember that is not an offense; we are, in fact, the more fragile vessel.

> *Likewise, husbands, live with your wives in an understanding way, showing honor to the woman as the weaker vessel, since they are heirs with you of the grace of life, so that your prayers may not be hindered.*
>
> — 1 Peter 3:7

When we have been disappointed and left feeling underappreciated, it can be difficult to maintain the strength we need. However, the much-needed strength will be supplied by God as we daily surrender our concerns and pain to Him. I strongly believe we have to be so grounded in Jesus that nothing can remove us from His truth. We need Jesus more now than ever; the lie of the enemy is that we are not enough. We then enter into relationships that do not have a strong foundation in Christ, and that weak foundation allows the enemy of our souls to creep in with his lies. The truth is we have been made with a purpose. That purpose is to demonstrate God's love, but in order to do that we must know God's truth. We need to be prepared in every season because it will not always be sunny, and the snow won't always fall softly.

Also make sure you are surrounded by godly women or one really good, prayerful friend. Someone you know loves the Lord and will cover you in prayer at any given time. Not the ones that will constantly make you feel that you are not perfect enough for God. That will take place when Jesus comes for His church. Find a godly friend who will be honest with you, always lead you in God's truth, and will never judge you but will instantly pray you through. That is also part of what helped me in my healing process. For as much as I wanted to keep my pain concealed from everyone, I realized it did me more harm than good.

> *Oil and perfume make the heart glad, and the sweetness of a friend comes from his earnest counsel.*
>
> — Proverbs 27:9

Remember to stay grounded in God's truth. Stay blessed.

www.ingramcontent.com/pod-product-compliance
Lightning Source LLC
Chambersburg PA
CBHW071340010225
21202CB00008B/111
* 9 7 9 8 8 9 3 3 3 8 5 0 8 *